THE SEASONS

Autumn

Ralph Whitlock

Titles in this series

Spring

Summer

Autumn

Winter

Edited by Andrew Kelly
Designed by Malcolm Smythe

First published in 1987 by
Wayland (Publishers) Ltd
61 Western Road, Hove
East Sussex BN3 1JD, England

© Copyright 1987 Wayland (Publishers) Ltd

British Library Cataloguing in Publication Data
Whitlock, Ralph
 Autumn.—(The Seasons)
 1. Autumn—Juvenile literature
 I. Title   II. Series
 574.5'43   QH81

HARDBACK ISBN 0–85078–841–2

PAPERBACK ISBN 0–7502–0561–X

Typeset by D.P. Press Limited, Sevenoaks
Printed and bound in Belgium by Casterman S.A.

Contents

What seasons are

Autumn is one of the four seasons of the temperate regions of the world. The other three are spring, summer and winter. Each season is marked by changes in the length of day and night, and each has a particular type of weather, although it takes many weeks for one season to change to the next.

There are natural dividing lines between the seasons called equinoxes and solstices. The equinoxes are the dates on which day and night are of equal length. They occur on 21 March,

In autumn young children love walking through the fallen leaves.

roughly the beginning of northern spring, and 23 September, the beginning of northern autumn.

Summer and winter are marked by periods called solstices. This is when there is the greatest difference between the length of day and night. In the northern hemisphere, the longest summer day is 21 June while the shortest winter day is about 21 December.

Nature responds to the changes in seasons and this is particularly noticeable with plants.

Seasons vary around the world. Near the equator it is always hot and often wet, and near the Poles it is always cold, though the temperature does rise for part of the year. As the chart below shows, seasons in the southern half of the world are the reverse of those in the northern half.

Northern Hemisphere			
Autumn	*Winter*	*Spring*	*Summer*
September	December	March	June
October	January	April	July
November	February	May	August
Spring	*Summer*	*Autumn*	*Winter*
Southern Hemisphere			

In the north there may be snow at Christmas, while people in the south may be having their Christmas dinner on a beach.

Right *In autumn many mornings are frosty.*

Why seasons happen

The earth spins like a top on its axis. Every twenty-four hours it completes one turn. As the earth turns, each part of the earth's surface comes into the sun's rays for a period of time and then turns away. This gives us day and night. Unlike a top, the axis (the line around which it spins) isn't vertical but tilted. It is this tilt which causes the seasons as the earth does its yearly orbit around the sun. The tilt is at the same angle all year. This means that different parts of the earth are closer to the sun at different times of the year.

On 21 March and 23 September, the sun is overhead at the equator. These are the spring and autumn equinoxes, when day and night are of equal length.

Between March and September, the North Pole is tilted towards the sun. The days are longer than the nights and the sun's rays are received more directly, so causing the warmer summer weather in the northern hemisphere. On 21 June, the sun is overhead at the Tropic of Cancer. This is the time of the summer solstice.

While it is summer in the northern hemisphere, the southern hemisphere is experiencing winter, because the South Pole is tilted away from the sun.

Six months later, the earth has moved to the opposite side of the sun, and at the time of the winter solstice,

Day and night
Every twenty-four hours the earth completes one turn about its axis. This rotation causes day and night.

Earth's axis

This diagram shows the earth at one of the equinoxes, with the sun overhead at the equator. Further away from the equator the sun is weaker, because the curvature of the earth causes the same amount of sunlight to be spread over a wider area and to pass through a greater thickness of atmosphere. The heat of the sun is therefore less strong in temperate regions and very weak in polar regions.

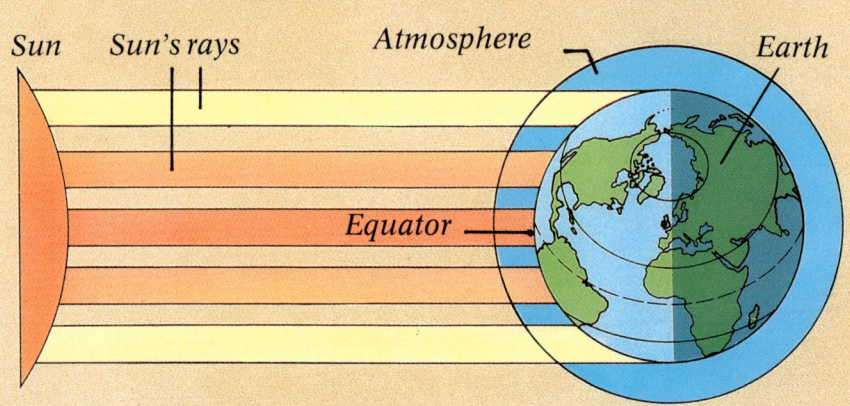

Sun   Sun's rays   Atmosphere   Earth

Equator

As autumn progresses, the sun sets earlier each evening.

21 December, the North Pole is tilted away from the sun. The sun is now directly over the Tropic of Capricorn. This then is the period of southern summer and northern winter.

Between the tropics and the equator, day and night are of roughly equal length and temperatures vary little between one part of the year and another. Beyond the Arctic and Antarctic Circles, the year more or less divides itself into two seasons, summer and winter. Only the places between the tropics and the Arctic and Antarctic Circles have the marked seasonal transitions of spring and autumn.

The spinning earth orbits the sun once a year. This diagram shows how the tilt of the earth affects the amount of light and heat reaching different parts of the earth at different times of year, so giving us the changing seasons.

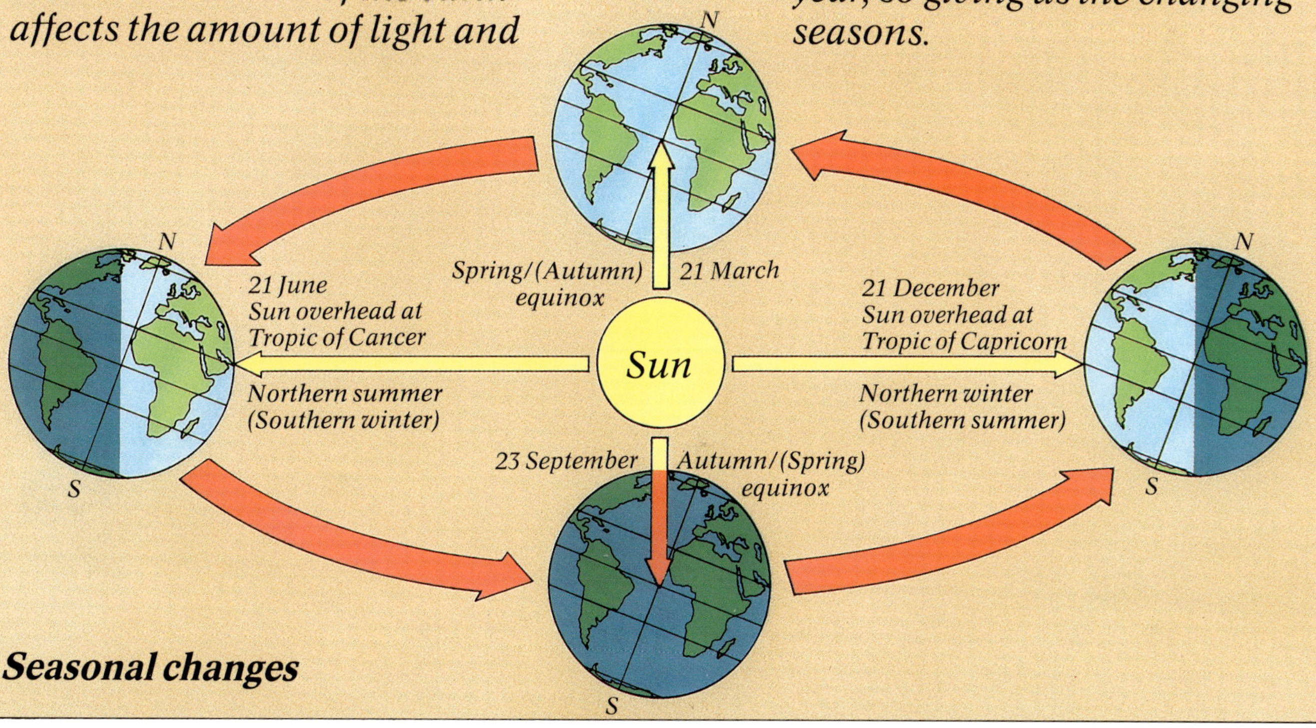

21 June
Sun overhead at
Tropic of Cancer

Northern summer
(Southern winter)

Spring/(Autumn)
equinox   21 March

Sun

21 December
Sun overhead at
Tropic of Capricorn

Northern winter
(Southern summer)

23 September   Autumn/(Spring)
equinox

Seasonal changes

Autumn around the world

Autumn is a season that occurs in the temperate regions of the world. Temperate means mild, and these regions do not have the extremes of polar cold or tropical heat.

Autumn is the season of diminishing sunlight. The sun doesn't rise as high in the sky each day and it sets earlier each evening. The days grow colder and colder. This is the period when animals, plants and people must prepare for the coming winter.

Farmers and gardeners gather their crops and store them for winter use. Deciduous trees cease to pump sap into their outermost twigs, thus allowing their leaves to die and fall to the ground. Most insects spend the winter in the form of eggs or pupae. This makes them immune to frosts. Some animals find places in which to hibernate and many birds migrate from their nesting territories to countries with warmer climates.

Yet autumn is also a season of plenty. Food is abundant and creatures make the best use of it. Migrating birds put on weight to sustain them for their long journey. Animals that hibernate accumulate layers of fat to see them through their winter sleep.

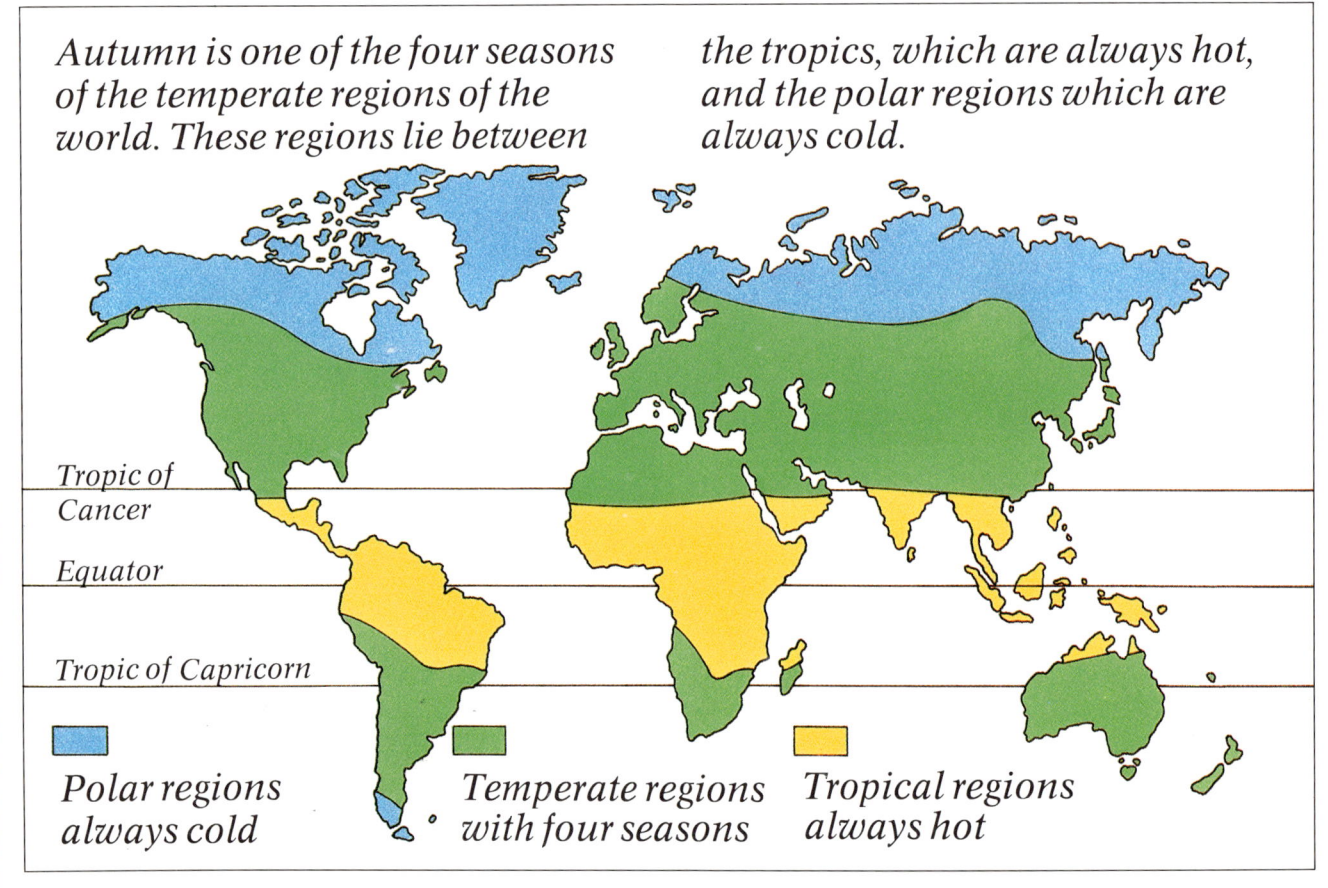

Autumn is one of the four seasons of the temperate regions of the world. These regions lie between the tropics, which are always hot, and the polar regions which are always cold.

Tropic of Cancer

Equator

Tropic of Capricorn

Polar regions always cold

Temperate regions with four seasons

Tropical regions always hot

A child in Kashmir, India, takes maize from the autumn harvest.

In many places autumn is a very lovely season. The leaves of deciduous trees in forests, orchards and gardens turn bronze, gold, crimson and red. Autumn colours are particularly impressive in the forests of Canada and northern USA.

Below *The forests of North America are noted for their brilliant autumn colours.*

Autumn weather

Autumn is warmer than spring because the land and the sea have been warmed by the summer sun and take time to cool. Gradually, however, as the days grow shorter, the nights become colder and we feel the approach of winter.

Autumn is a season of storms in many places, especially in the northern hemisphere. Towards the end of the summer, the prolonged heat causes masses of hot air to build up into towering mountains of cloud in the tropics. These menacing clouds tend to move with a circular motion, creating vast funnels of air often several miles high. As they move over the oceans they draw up quantities of water and so develop into huge tropical storms, known as hurricanes, cyclones or typhoons.

These storms can move quickly, covering huge distances and leaving great destruction behind them. They often move out of the tropics and into the temperate zones. Many storms develop in the Gulf of Mexico and move northward. They are often still capable of great destruction when they reach New York.

Fogs are common in autumn and are produced in many different ways. One

Typhoons occur in autumn and can cause much damage.

Fog is common in autumn.

way, which frequently happens in autumn, is that the cold ground cools the air above, so the water vapour in the air forms many tiny water droplets. It is these water droplets, suspended in the air because they are too light to fall to the ground, that make fog look white.

Autumn is the time when the first frosts appear in many parts of the world. Frost is frozen dew. In the cooler parts of the temperate regions, the first heavy or 'killing' frost of autumn marks the end of the growing season for many plants, including most crops.

Below *There are many frosts in autumn. This is hoar frost.*

Autumn weather is very changeable. Some days can be warm and sunny.

Birds and animals in autumn

In autumn all wild creatures know instinctively that cold weather is coming. They know they must either prepare for it where they are or seek to escape from it.

Those best able to flee from it are birds, for they are equipped with wings which enable them to fly long distances – towards the tropics and away from the icy polar winds. Perhaps the most obvious of the bird migrations in the northern hemisphere are those of swallows and martins, familiar birds which assemble in big flocks on telephone and electricity lines as they prepare for their tremendous journey to the south. Many European swallows travel across the tropics to spend winter in South Africa.

Nearly all the vast numbers of birds that nest in the Arctic move

In autumn caribou migrate south from the Arctic tundra to the forest zone.

southwards, though many do not go as far as the tropics but winter in the temperate zone.

In the southern hemisphere the movements are, of course, northwards. The sacred kingfisher, for instance, travels from southern Australia to Malaya; and certain hummingbirds fly north from Tierra del Fuego to tropical America.

Some animals also escape from winter by migrating. The most spectacular migrations are those of the caribou, which feed on the Arctic tundra in summer but retreat to the forest zone in autumn. Sometimes as many as 50,000 caribou are to be seen in a single herd.

In autumn many animals prepare to spend the winter in hibernation. Hibernation enables animals to survive even when there is little food around. It is a special form of sleep. The body of the hibernating animal becomes very cool and all its bodily processes, such as breathing, slow down. In this state the animal uses very little energy.

During autumn, when food is abundant, animals such as dormice and bats become very fat, but they will use most of this fat during their winter sleep. Autumn is also the time when an animal must find a sheltered hiding place to hibernate in – a burrow, a nest or perhaps a hollow log. Frogs and turtles often bury themselves in the mud at the bottom of ponds.

The sacred kingfisher migrates from southern Australia in autumn.

Below *This vole is collecting berries to store for the winter.*

13

Insects in autumn

Insects, which have been multiplying all the summer, are extremely abundant in autumn. During the summer they have been the food supply for the young of most small birds. In autumn the adult birds eat them, to fatten themselves up for the winter. Most insects come to a violent end, by being eaten by some creature or other, but enough survive to ensure a new generation next spring.

Like other animals, insects face the problem of surviving the cold winter weather, and autumn is the season in which they must make their preparations.

In autumn, caterpillars can be found. This is a swallowtail caterpillar.

Moths and butterflies begin life as eggs which hatch into caterpillars. These change into pupae, from which the adults finally emerge.

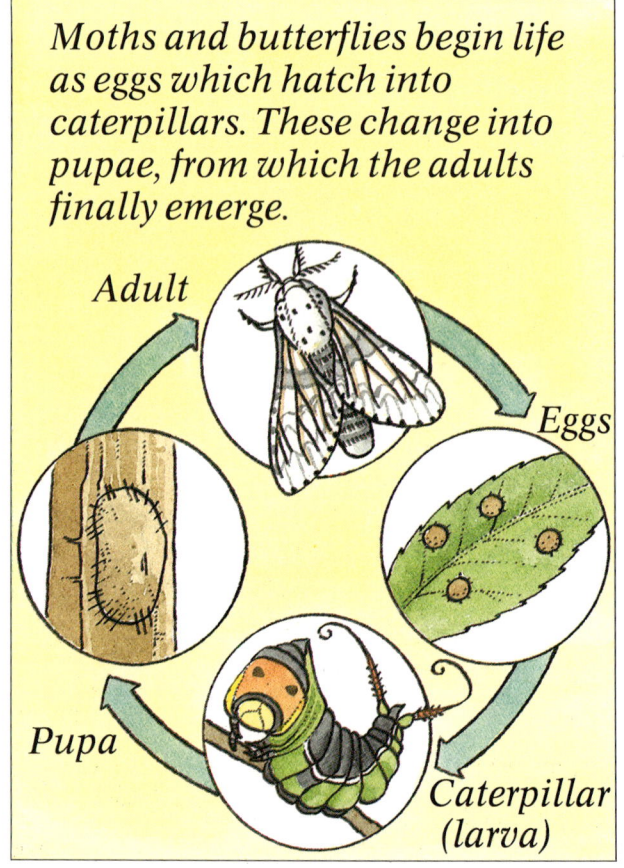

Adult

Eggs

Pupa

Caterpillar (larva)

Fortunately for insects, during two of their four stages of life they are immune to winter weather. As eggs and as pupae they are not even aware of the cold. Many of them spend the summer in the larval stage, eating as much as they can and growing fast, so that by autumn the countryside swarms with caterpillars, grubs, maggots and other larvae. Autumn is the season to look for big, spectacular, fully-grown caterpillars.

For adult insects feeding is not usually so important. Some of them do not eat at all. Their role is to breed and also to search for new sites to colonize.

Spider webs are common in autumn.

Some insects are celebrated migrants. Many migrate towards the warmer tropic regions. One of the most remarkable is the monarch, or milkweed, butterfly of North America, which both migrates and hibernates. Some monarchs fly from Quebec to Mexico, over 3,000 km.

In response to the vast increase of insects in summer, the creatures which prey on them also increase. The autumn countryside swarms with spiders, which spin webs that look like silken blankets covering everything.

Migration of the monarch butterfly
In autumn the monarch butterfly leaves Canada and northern USA and migrates towards the southwestern states and Mexico.

The butterflies form huge swarms which settle on trees (below, left) and spend the mild winter in a state of partial hibernation. In early March they fly north again.

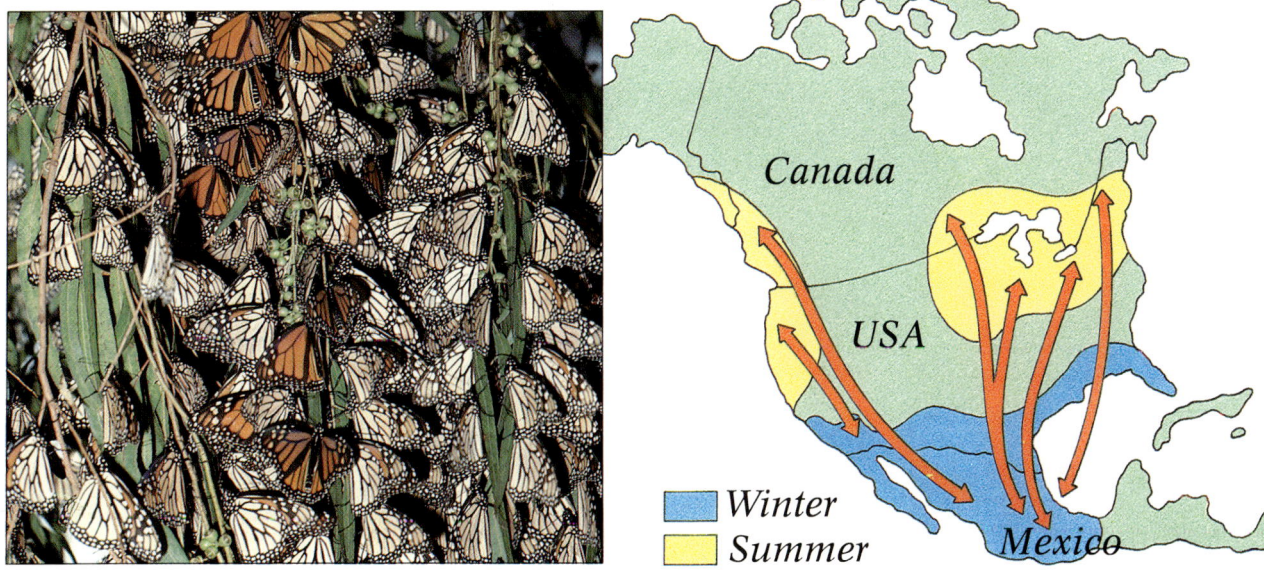

Canada

USA

Winter
Summer

Mexico

Plants in autumn

The most noticeable thing about plants in autumn is the colour of the leaves of deciduous trees. In spring and summer the trees produce a lot of chlorophyll, the substance that gives leaves their green colour. In autumn this chlorophyll is gradually lost from the leaves, and they turn yellow or brown. Some leaves are bright red because sugar gets trapped in them just before they fall to the ground.

Deciduous trees lose their leaves in autumn to protect themselves against the winter cold. The sap, which is the life of the trees, retreats into the roots, and the trees become dormant in much the same way as hibernating

In autumn the leaves of deciduous trees turn red, yellow and brown.

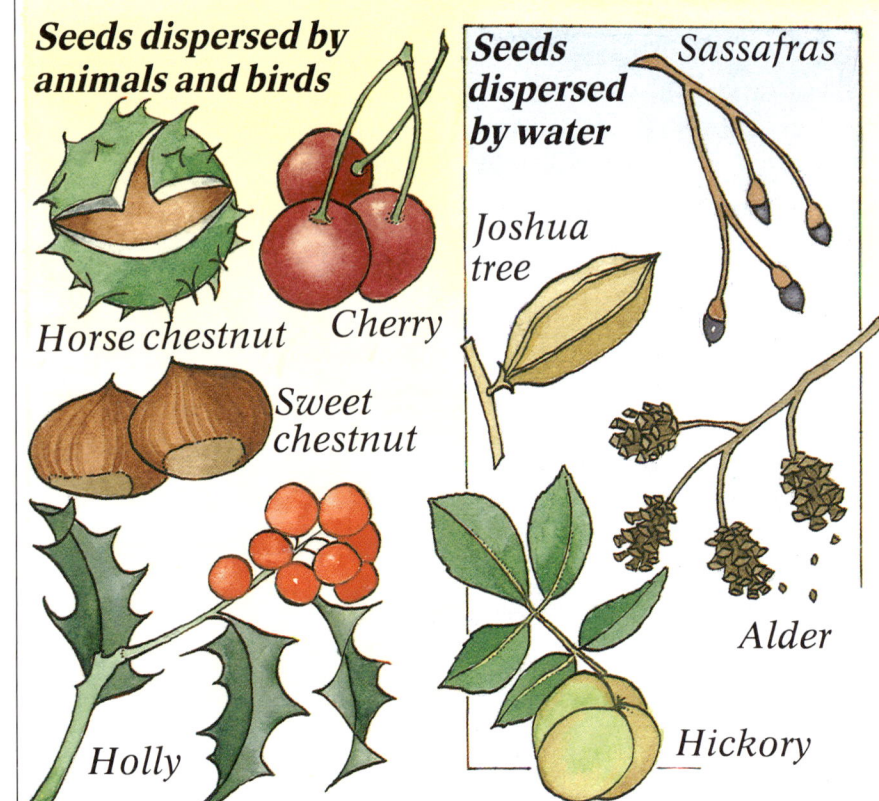

Seeds dispersed by animals and birds

Horse chestnut

Cherry

Sweet chestnut

Holly

Seeds dispersed by water

Sassafras

Joshua tree

Alder

Hickory

Seed dispersal
To have the best chance to grow, seeds need to be carried far from the parent plant. Some seeds are inside fruit and nuts which are eaten by birds and animals who deposit the seeds elsewhere. The seeds of other plants are carried away by the wind. These seeds are often large but light. Still other plants use flowing water to carry their seeds away.

Ivy is one of the last plants to flower in autumn.

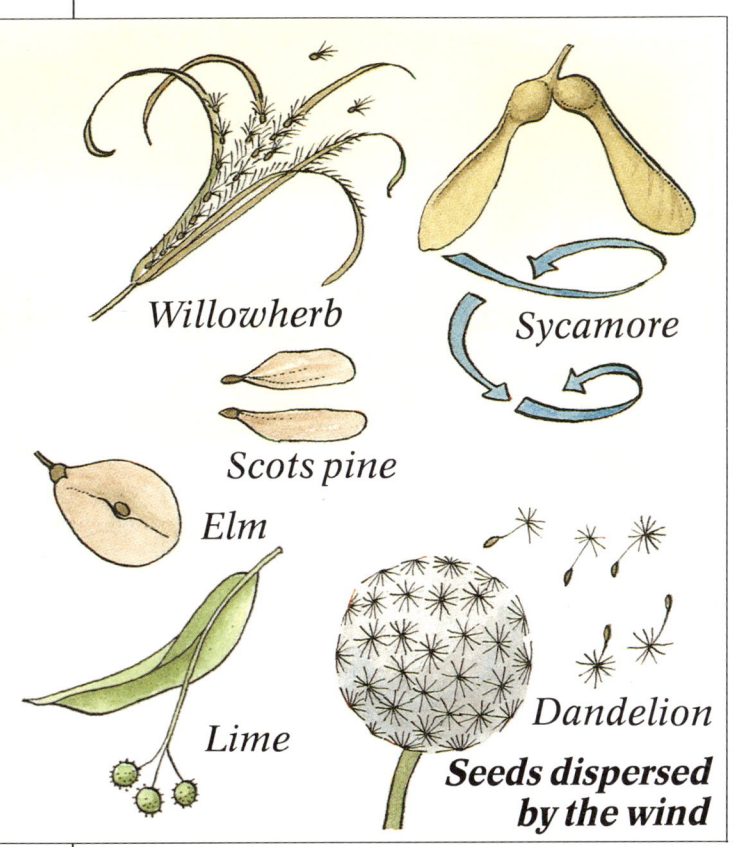

Willowherb

Sycamore

Scots pine

Elm

Lime

Dandelion

Seeds dispersed by the wind

animals. The discarded leaves fall to the ground and, as they rot, they are incorporated into the soil. Evergreen trees that keep their leaves all year stop growing in autumn and don't produce any new growth till the following spring.

Some plants, called annuals, die after they have flowered. However, before they die they release seeds which fall to the ground or are carried away by the wind or by animals. Some seeds fall into rivers or streams and are carried away by water. Eventually the seeds settle in the soil where, during the following spring, they will grow and flower.

For most plants and trees, autumn is the time when seeds are released to produce a new generation.

Crop farming in autumn

Most of the crops grown by farmers are annuals. In most of the temperate parts of the world, these ripen for harvesting in autumn. The most important are cereal crops, which include wheat, barley, rice and maize (corn), and are valued for their seed. They are really kinds of grasses, and they follow the usual life cycle of grasses, producing first leaves, then flower stems and finally seeds. The farmer gathers the ripe seeds and stores them for winter use or sells them for making bread and other foods.

In the parts of the temperate zones nearest the tropics, the hot sun causes seeds to ripen quickly, and many crops are ready for harvest in summer. The farther one travels away from the tropics the later the harvest. On the edge of the Arctic getting the crops harvested and stored before the onset of winter is often a struggle. Maize (corn) in particular ripens late in cool climates. Modern machinery, notably the combine harvester, enables farmers to complete their harvest more quickly than in the days when cereals

A combine harvester in northern Iowa, USA, harvesting maize (corn).

This farmer is preparing the ground for autumn sowing.

had to be cut with scythes or sickles and collected by hand.

Harvesting the crops used to be such a tremendous undertaking that its completion was the grand climax of the year, celebrated by a feast. Nowadays celebrating usually has to be postponed, for farmers have other things to do. There are new varieties of wheat and barley that have to be sown in autumn. If they can make adequate growth before hard weather comes they can survive severe frosts in winter. So the farmer tries to give his crops a good start by sowing the seed early.

Autumn vegetables

Many vegetables are ready for harvesting in autumn. Frost-sensitive vegetables must be harvested before the first cold spells arrive. Other vegetables can be left till later. Some autumn vegetables are the second crop of the year, while others have taken all summer to grow.

Runner beans   Potatoes   Beetroot   Cabbage   Carrots   Parsnip

Autumn – season of fruit and nuts

Except for soft fruits (such as strawberries, raspberries and currants) which ripen in summer, most fruits in temperate climates ripen in autumn. Apples, plums and pears are abundant in most parts of both the northern and southern temperate zones. Peaches, apricots, nectarines and citrus fruits (such as oranges and lemons) flourish only in regions which enjoy a Mediterranean climate. These include California, South Africa, Australia and temperate South America.

Grapes do not like the wet, windy climate of north-western Europe, but in dryer, inland regions they grow as far north as the Rhine valley in Germany. The grape harvest is an extremely important one, especially of the varieties of grapes used for making wine. Grapevines are now grown in all countries with a suitable climate. In recent years, wines made from Australian and Californian grapes have established a good reputation.

Picking fruit is one of the more enjoyable tasks on a farm or in a garden. Each apple, plum, pear, peach or apricot is individually selected and plucked with care, to ensure that the dust-like coating, or 'bloom', is not damaged. This is particularly important if the fruit is to be eaten as a dessert or stored, but not so necessary if it is to be used for making jam or fruit pulp. Apples used for making cider are now removed from the trees by a mechanical shaker.

In some countries, nuts of various sorts are grown as a commercial crop. They are usually left on the trees or bushes until they are quite ripe, when they will fall off or can be shaken off. Some kinds of nuts, however, grow wild in temperate climates and during rambles in the woods on sunny autumn afternoons, people often 'go nutting'.

As soon as fruit-picking is over, the fruit farmer prunes his trees and bushes and examines them for disease or damage, spraying them with chemicals if necessary.

Unusual garden fruits
The fruits of medlar, quince and persimmon are often cooked to make jellies and preserves.

Medlar

Passion fruit

Quince

Persimmon

Left *Apples ripen in autumn and many are made into cider.*

Below *Autumn is the time of the grape harvest. These grapes from the Dordogne in France will be turned into wine.*

Farm animals in autumn

Just as wild creatures instinctively prepare for winter, by migrating, hibernating or by laying-up stores of food in autumn, so provision has to be made for farm animals during the cold months. As they are unable to do this for themselves, farmers have to provide for them. Some of the farm cereal crops, notably barley and oats, are grown mainly as winter food for farm animals.

In order to avoid using up his stored food too quickly, the farmer keeps his animals in the fields for as long as possible. Immediately after the harvest he sows quick-growing crops, such as rye, for the cattle and sheep to graze before the severe weather comes.

As autumn advances, the field rations have to be supplemented by hay, cereal meal and silage (green crops stored as fodder). Eventually all but the hardiest animals are housed inside for the winter. In parts of North America and Australia, cattle and sheep are allowed to graze freely all summer, and may be brought into stockyards for feeding towards the end

Autumn is round-up time for cattle in many parts of the USA.

22

These sheep are feeding on turnips and rape planted after the harvest.

of autumn. Alternatively, hay and other feed may be fed to them in the fields. Many animals that were taken up to graze in the mountains in spring are brought down to their winter pastures in the lowlands.

Normally more young animals are born in summer than the farmer wants to keep through the winter. So in autumn there are many sales of farm animals. In Europe these often take the form of great fairs on traditional sites, where vast numbers of animals are sold.

Below *Many cattle sales, like this one in Scotland, are held in autumn.*

Autumn religious festivals

The autumn harvest is the climax of the farming year and is traditionally marked by a harvest festival. Country people used to celebrate the safe gathering into store of their crops, so ensuring their food supply for the coming year. When celebrated as a Christian religious festival it is known as Harvest Thanksgiving and is marked by special services in churches and by the singing of harvest hymns.

Most religions have similar festivals to celebrate a successful harvest. The Jewish Feast of Tabernacles, or *Succot*, is an eight-day festival held in September or October, at the end of the harvest. The tabernacles are tents or booths, decorated with fruits and flowers, where families live for a whole week of rejoicing.

The Hindus have a festival, called *Dasera*, which takes place after the harvest and after the early autumn seed-time of the rainy season in India. This is a period of clear, pleasant weather. Eighteen days later there is

---

The Harvest Festival

In many parts of Europe, autumn is the time when the Harvest Festival is celebrated. Churches are decorated with flowers, fruit and vegetables. In the front of the church, around the altar or pulpit, are more gifts of garden produce, brought by members of the church.

Left *These people are celebrating Succot in Jerusalem.*

another festival, *Diwali*, or the Festival of Lights, when every window is illuminated by lamps or candles, and homes are decorated with garlands of flowers. The Sikhs and Jains of India also celebrate *Diwali*.

Autumn in Southeast Asia is a period of very heavy rains, and people spend much of their time indoors. However, they do venture out for the festival of *Kathina* in October or November, when they take gifts to the monks in the monasteries.

Below *A flower-seller in Nepal. Hindus decorate their homes with flowers at* Diwali.

Huge models of a devil called Ravanna will be burnt during Dasera.

Special autumn days

When the Pilgrim Fathers landed from their ship the *Mayflower* at Plymouth, Massachusetts, in 1620, the date was 10 November. It was too late in autumn for sowing and preparing for a harvest, so times were hard until the following summer. By July 1621, however, it was clear to them that their first harvest was going to be a success. They were going to have enough food to see them through the next winter. So they decreed that 21 July should be a Thanksgiving Day. Thanksgiving Day is still celebrated throughout the USA, but it is now

This parade in Pacific Grove, California, marks the arrival of the migrant monarch butterflies.

held on the last Thursday in November. In Canada it is celebrated on the second Monday in October. Japan has also chosen a Labour Thanksgiving Day, which is on 23 November. Tokens of the harvest are presented on an altar built for the purpose.

An autumn festival that is very popular in many countries is Hallowe'en. Held on 31 October, it is derived from an old Celtic festival, *Samhain*, when the barrier between this world and the spiritual world was supposed to wear very thin, thus allowing ghosts and spirits to roam loose in the world. It was thought all manner of supernatural events were likely to occur. It was an occasion when bonfires were lit to ward off evil spirits. Children now celebrate Hallowe'en by making lanterns out of hollowed-out pumpkins and by going trick-or-treating. Trick-or-treating involves children going from house to house demanding a treat or, if it is not forthcoming, threatening to perform a harmless practical joke.

In Britain, Australia and New Zealand, the bonfires of Hallowe'en have become associated with Bonfire Night (5 November), or Guy Fawkes Night as it is sometimes called. This night commemorates the failure of an attempt to blow up the English Parliament in 1605. The attempt was called the Gunpowder Plot and one member of the plot was a gentleman called Guy Fawkes.

Below On Guy Fawkes Night there are fireworks displays, such as this one at Leeds Castle in England.

Right This person in fancy dress is at a Hallowe'en party in New York.

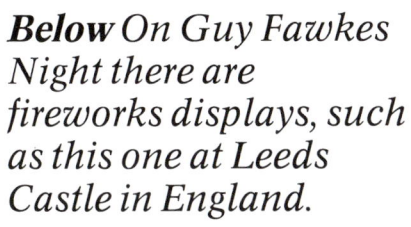

Autumn folklore

Early autumn is traditionally a time of rejoicing after a successful harvest. Before the Harvest Home Feast, farm labourers used to hoist the last sheaf on a prong and raise the time-honoured harvest shout:

Well ploughed,
Well sowed,
Well harrowed,
Well mowed,
And all safely carted to the barn
*   with never a load throwed!*
Hip-hip-hip-hooray!

The same spirit is evoked by the familiar harvest hymn, sung at most church harvest festivals:

Come, ye thankful people, come,
Raise the song of Harvest Home;
All is safely gathered in
Ere the winter storms begin . . .

Some of the liveliest songs associated with harvest are drinking songs. Autumn marches on to Hallowe'en, the time of ghosts and spirits. In some places in England it was known as Punkie Night, a 'punkie' being a will-o'-the-wisp, thought to be a lost spirit. So children, keeping close together for company and carrying muppet-like lanterns, still chant:

It's Punkie Night tonight;
It's Punkie Night tonight;
Give us a candle; give us a light,
For it's Punkie Night tonight.

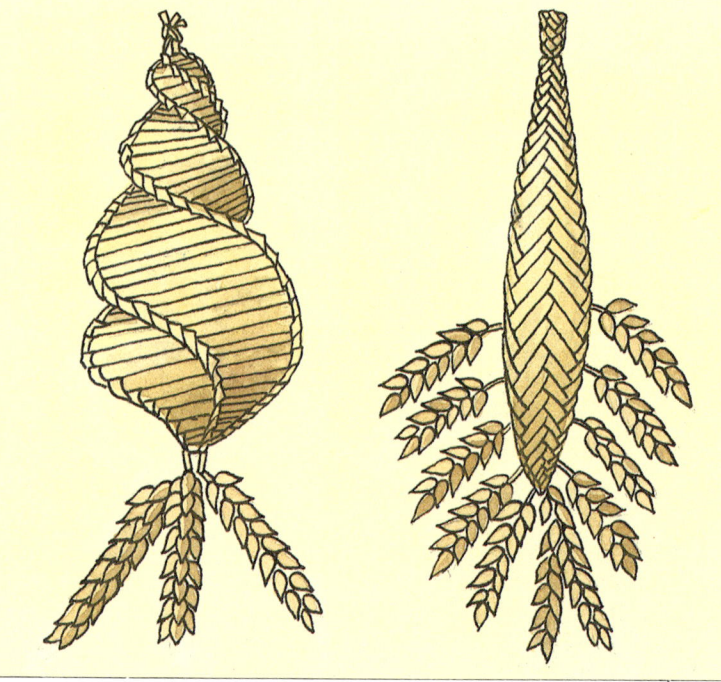

These men, who are wearing traditional French folk costumes, are showing how the harvest was done in the past.

Many of the sayings associated with autumn are concerned with the weather:

Ice in November to bear a duck;
Nothing afterwards but slush and muck.

And it is true that hard frosts in autumn are usually followed by a wet, muddy period. A parallel saying promises:

A wet November, a plentiful year.

A piece of agricultural wisdom is contained in the couplet:

In early autumn dung your field,
And your land its wealth will yield.

Corn dollies

These are examples of corn dollies. In the past the corn goddess was thought to live in the last few stalks to be harvested. They were reverently cut and woven into her image. Now they are purely ornamental. The man (far left) is weaving a corn dolly.

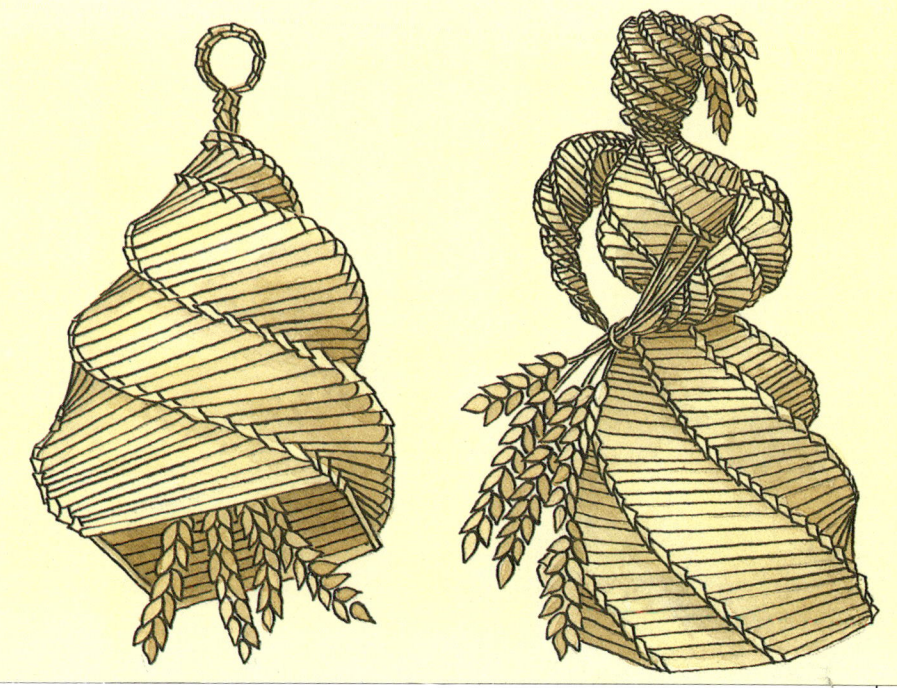

Autumn in literature

Probably the best-known poem on the subject of autumn in the English language is John Keats's 'Ode to Autumn'. It begins:

*Season of mists and mellow
    fruitfulness!
Close bosom-friend of the
    maturing sun;
Conspiring with him how to load
    and bless
With fruit the vines that round the
    thatch-eaves run;
To bend with apples the moss'd
    cottage-trees,
And fill all fruit with ripeness to
    the core;*

*To swell the gourd and plump the
    hazel shells
With a sweet kernel, to set budding
    more,
And still more, later flowers for the
    bees,
Until they think warm days will
    never cease,
For Summer has o'er brimmed
    their clammy cells . . .*

He goes on to describe other features of a quiet autumn day: the amber-coloured apple juices oozing from cider-presses; full-grown lambs bleating; hedge-crickets singing; swallows 'twittering in the skies'.

It is this sort of scene that has inspired people to write about autumn.

A Canadian poet, Wilfred Campbell, celebrates the beauty of the Canadian autumn, when the forests turn crimson and gold, in the following poem called 'Indian Summer':

Along the line of smoky hills
The crimson forest stands,
And all the day the blue-jay calls
Throughout the autumn lands.

Now by the brook the maple
*   leans*
With all his glory spread,
And all the sumachs on the hills
Have turned their green to red.

Now by great marshes wrapt in
*   mist,*
Or past some river's mouth,
Throughout the long, still autumn
*   day*
Wild birds are flying south.

And Tennyson puts into graphic lines the end of the English autumn:

Tonight the winds begin to rise
And roar from yonder dropping
*   day;*
The last red leaf is whirl'd away,
The rooks are blown about the
*   skies. . . .*

31

Autumn in art

Autumn is not as popular a subject among artists as the other seasons. The flowers of spring, the sunlight of summer and the starkness of winter snow have an immediate appeal to the artist's eye. Autumn with its subtle tones is a more difficult subject to paint. Some artists, using these tones, have produced great works of art about autumn. In many pictures the reds, bronzes, golds and yellows of the autumn leaves dominate the composition. The harvest is a very popular subject in paintings of autumn.

Below *'The Seine at Argenteuil, Autumn' by Claude Monet.*

Above *A detail from 'The Haywain' by John Constable.*

'Allee des Alyscamps' by Vincent Van Gogh.

Autumn clothes

Generally, the clothes we wear in summer are as light as possible, whereas in winter we need plenty of waterproof clothing to keep us warm and dry. Autumn is the season of transition between the two. The change is gradual, like all seasonal changes. At first we hardly notice we have moved from summer into autumn. Perhaps we just have to wear our raincoats more frequently, because it rains more often. Soon, though, we find we want to pull on our gloves in the mornings, and by the end of the autumn we are wrapping scarves around our necks and wearing overcoats and warm boots.

We are luckier than our grandparents in having clothes made of nylon and other synthetic fabrics. These are usually windproof, so we do not need to wear numerous layers of thick clothes which restrict our movements. Clothes not only form a barrier against low temperatures around us, they also help to prevent our body heat from escaping. Synthetics are very efficient in doing this. Much body heat is lost through the head, so in cold weather it is important to wear a hat.

Most sports now have their own special gear. For energetic outdoor sports, such as football and cross-country running, we wear a basic minimum of clothes. It is important, though, to wash and change when the exercise is over.

Below and **left** In chilly autumn weather we must wear clothes that keep us warm and dry.

Autumn recreations and sports

Autumn is the season of overlap between the busy summer schedule of sports and other outdoor activities and the winter programme of largely indoor events. The cricket season is finishing as autumn begins. Traditionally, the soccer season in Britain (where the game originated) started when the cricket season ended, but League Football has now encroached on the season of summer sports by starting in August. In many countries, of course, football is not a seasonal sport and is played all year.

By the second month of autumn, the weather is considered too uncertain and the days too short for some outdoor events. International golf tournaments and international tennis matches take place on the other side of the world, where the seasons are reversed. Water sports are phased out as the seas and lakes become too chilly for comfort for most people, though some continue to sail, water ski and dive all winter.

Summer sports tend to be leisurely, but autumn sports need to be

A sailing regatta in early autumn in Auckland Harbour, New Zealand.

Many people keep fit by jogging.

energetic, allowing those taking part to keep warm. Rambling, jogging, orienteering and cross-country running are becoming very popular.

Traditional country sports are mostly blood sports. They include fox-hunting and the shooting of pheasants, partridges, hares and wildfowl. In Britain, a good deal of colourful pageantry is attached to fox-hunting, and crowds often assemble to watch a meet of the hounds. But many people think that blood sports are cruel and unnecessary.

Autumn can be a good time to go hiking. These people are hiking in Alaska.

Things to do – studying nature

Keeping a nature diary
In autumn, as well as during the other seasons of the year, you can keep a nature diary. Unlike spring and summer, few flowers bloom in autumn but you can record those that do. Among the last of all flowers to bloom are those of ivy.

You can also record the behaviour of migrating birds. You may see swallows and martins, collecting in flocks and perching on electricity and telephone lines just before they migrate. You may also notice birds, not usually found in your area, on their way to the places where they will winter.

There are many insects in autumn. You can record what they are, where they are found and what they feed on. It is also interesting to note the weather conditions at the time you see them, for example, is it sunny or overcast?

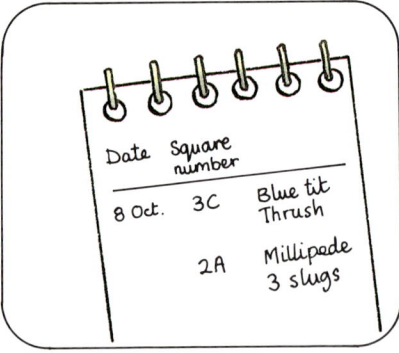

One way to study nature is to draw a map of your garden and then divide it into equal squares. Along one side write numbers next to each square; along another side write letters. Each day write down what you see in your garden and in which square you see it. You will notice that some things are only found in certain parts of the garden.

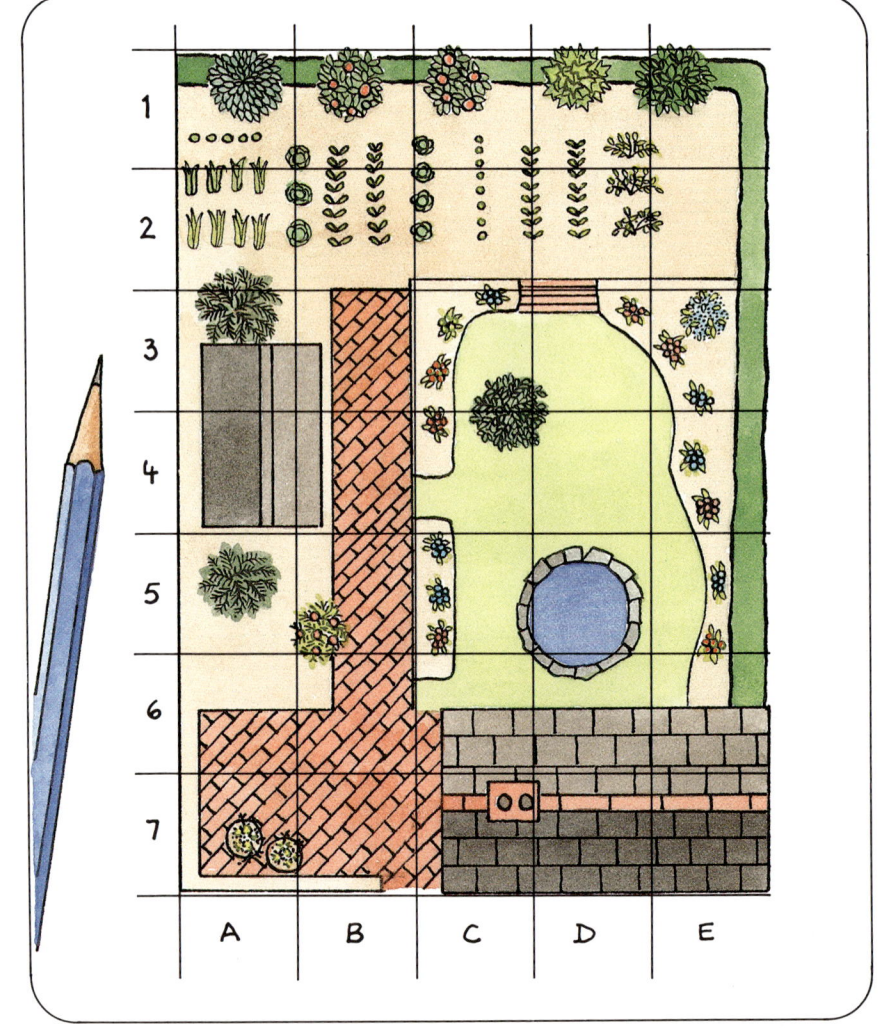

Seed and berry collection

You may like to make a collection of seeds and berries. If you want to grow some of them next spring, place each variety of seed in a separate envelope, label it, and store it in a dry cupboard or drawer. Keep the seeds in the open for a few days at first though, to make sure they are properly dry.

Cornflower

Poppy

Convolvulus

Poppy seeds

Growing a tree seed

Collect some tree seeds (but throw away any that are small or damaged). Soak a seed in warm water.

Put some stones in the bottom of a flower pot and half fill it with moist soil. Put the seed in the pot and cover it with more soil. At first keep a plastic bag over the pot to keep the soil damp. Later, when you have removed the bag, remember to water the seedling regularly. Also remember that plants need plenty of light.

Beech and oak seeds grow quite quickly but others take several months to appear. Plant different types of tree seeds at the same time and compare their progress.

Plastic bag

Beech seedling

String

Beech nuts

39

Things to do – studying the weather

The Beaufort Scale

It is often very windy in autumn. You can estimate the speed of the wind using the Beaufort Scale, which was devised by Sir Francis Beaufort in 1805. The Scale with the appropriate signs to look for is shown below.

N	Description	Wind speed kph	mph	Common signs for recognition
0	Calm	0–1.6	0–1	Smoke rises vertically.
1	Light air	3.2–4.8	2–3	Smoke slowly drifts.
2	Light breeze	6.4–11.3	4–7	Wind felt on face; leaves just move.
3	Gentle breeze	12.8–17.7	8–11	Flags flap; leaves move continuously.
4	Moderate breeze	19.3–25.7	12–16	Paper blows; dust raised; small branches move.
5	Fresh breeze	27.4–33.8	17–21	Small trees in leaf sway.
6	Strong breeze	35.4–43.5	22–27	Branches on trees move.
7	Moderate gale	45.1–53.1	28–33	Whole trees sway.
8	Fresh gale	54.7–64.4	34–40	Twigs and small branches break off. Gale warnings on radio.
9	Strong gale	66.0–77.3	41–48	Large branches break off. Slight damage to property.
10	Whole gale	78.9–90.2	49–56	Trees uprooted; major damage.
11	Storm	91.8–104.7	57–65	Usually at sea; widespread damage.
12	Hurricane	106.3+	66+	Usually at sea or coastal areas in tropics. Disaster conditions.

Making an anemometer

You can also measure the speed of the wind by making an anemometer.

You need a small spirit level, a protractor, a piece of thread, some tape, glue and a table-tennis ball. Tape the spirit level to the straight edge of the protractor. (If your spirit level is like the one in the diagram, it can be hooked over the edge of the protractor.) Then glue one end of the thread to the table-tennis ball. Tape the other end of the thread to the middle of the protractor so that the thread hangs down at 0°. Hold your anemometer into the wind. Make sure it is level and then read the angle which the table-tennis ball pulls the thread up to when blown by the wind. Use this angle to calculate the wind speed from the chart (opposite).

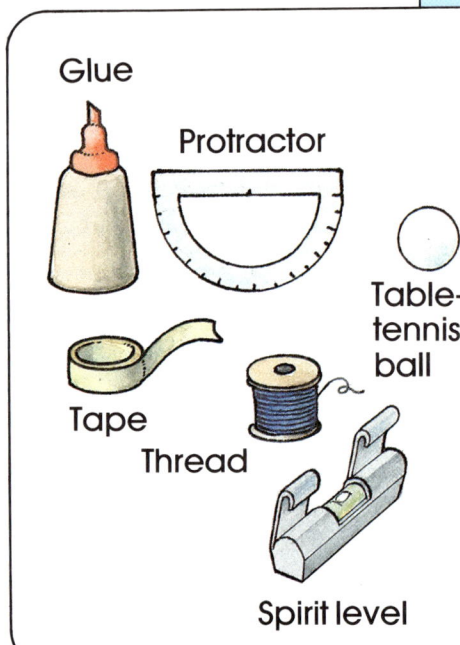

Glue

Protractor

Table-tennis ball

Tape

Thread

Spirit level

Making a rain gauge

You can keep a record of the rainfall using a home-made rain gauge. Find a plastic funnel and a glass jar that are the same width. The top of the funnel should be just a little larger than the mouth of the jar. Draw a metric or inch scale on a piece of paper and glue this scale to the outside of the jar so that the scale faces inward. Cover the scale with a piece of sticky plastic sheet. Place your rain gauge outside. Record the amount of rain in your rain gauge at about the same time every day. After each reading you must empty your rain gauge.

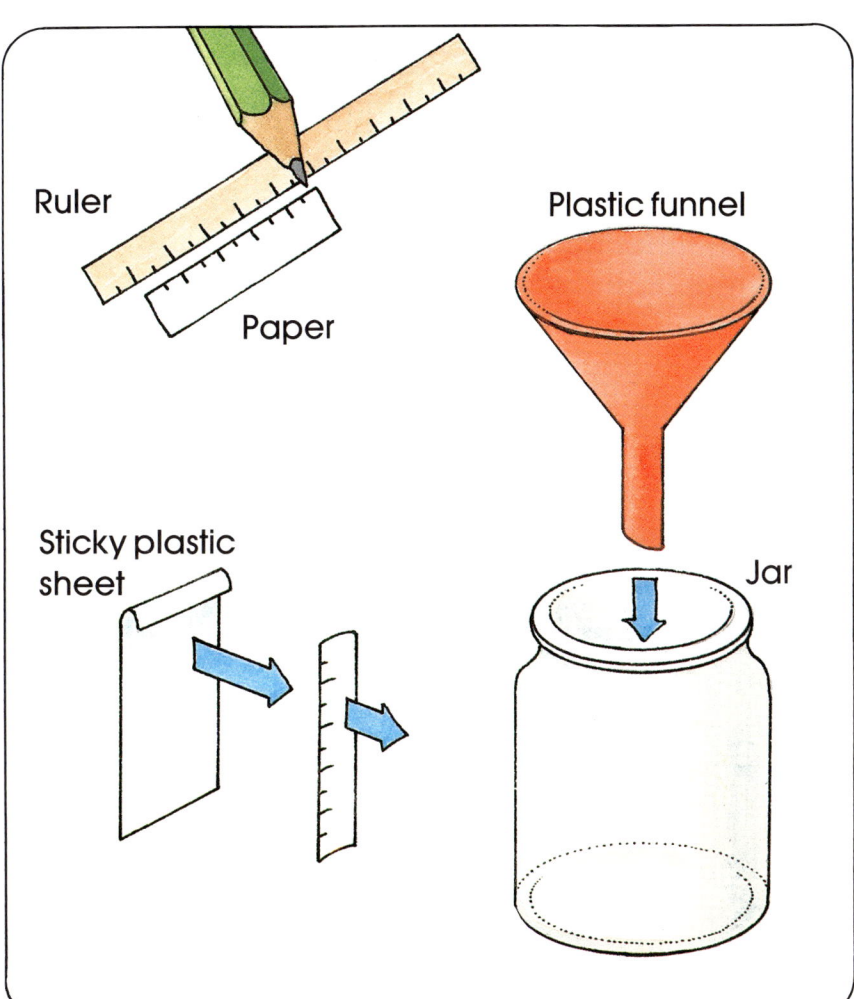

Ruler

Paper

Plastic funnel

Sticky plastic sheet

Jar

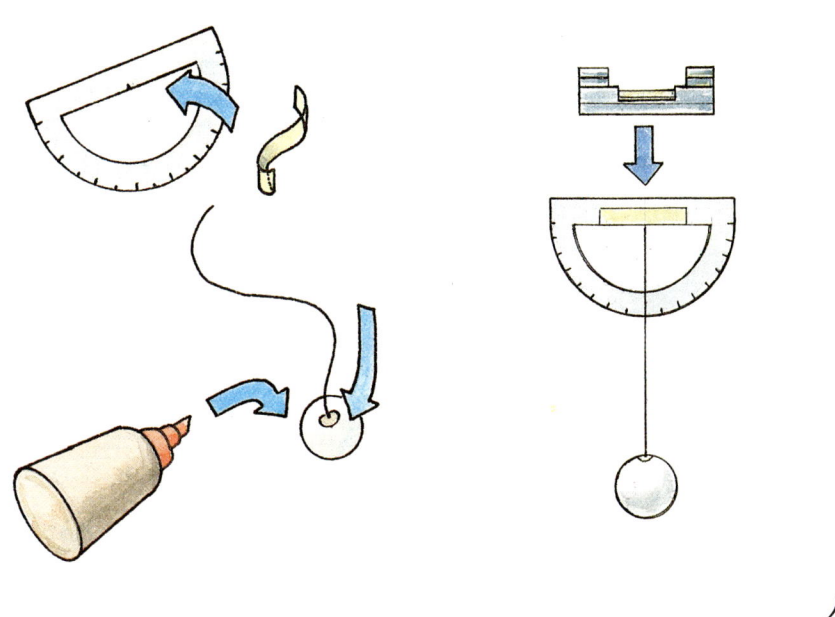

Wind-speed chart		
Angle	**Kph**	**Mph**
90°	0	0
85°	9.3	5.8
80°	13.2	8.2
75°	16.3	10.1
70°	19.0	11.8
65°	21.6	13.4
60°	24.0	14.9
55°	26.4	16.4
50°	29.0	18.0
45°	31.5	19.6
40°	34.4	21.4
35°	37.6	23.4
30°	41.5	25.8
25°	46.2	28.7
20°	52.3	32.5

Things to do with food

Here are some things to make in autumn. **Ask an adult to help before you begin.**

Tisane

A tisane is a herb tea. In autumn, many herbs are ready for gathering and drying. Gather small bunches and hang them upside-down on a line in a cool, airy room. When they are thoroughly dry, strip off the leaves and store them in small, opaque, sealed containers. To make a tisane crumble the dried herbs into a teapot and add boiling water, just as you would with tea-leaves or tea-bags. You can use a single herb, such as mint or camomile, or a mixture of several, or you can mix some of the herb leaves with tea-leaves. Use sugar, if you like your drinks sweet, but never add milk or cream.

Mint

Camomile

Fennel

Lemon balm

Frumenty

It is harvest time on farms. Maybe you will be able to visit a harvest field and find some of the ears of wheat which have fallen on the ground; or perhaps the farmer will give you a handful of wheat. Try making frumenty with it. You wash the wheat first, then half fill a jar with it. Cover the wheat with milk and set in a warm (not hot) oven for twelve hours. The grains will swell and burst and can be eaten straight away with cream and sugar. You can take the process a stage further by boiling the grains with milk, sultanas, and spices.

Hallowe'en lantern

Carefully cut the top off a pumpkin and scoop out the flesh. Then cut out eyes, nose and mouth for a face, stick some matchsticks in the mouth to represent teeth, and fix a candle inside. Then replace the top.

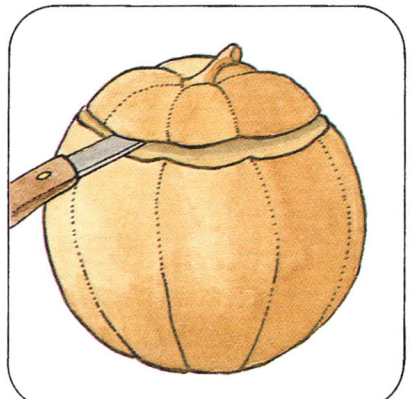

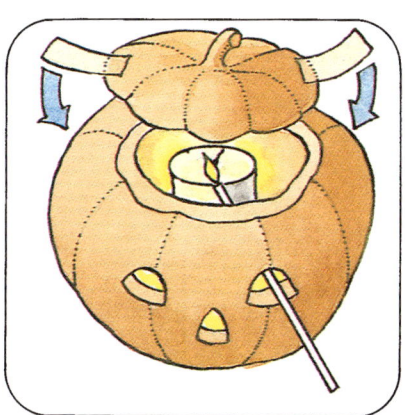

Pumpkin seeds

Don't waste the seeds from the pumpkin you used to make the lantern. Clean them first; then put them in a shallow pan, sprinkle with salt and roast them. Stir them occasionally and you will find that when they are dry and crisp they are delicious. If you don't want to eat the seeds, dry them and make a necklace. Or make seed pictures by sticking them on card.

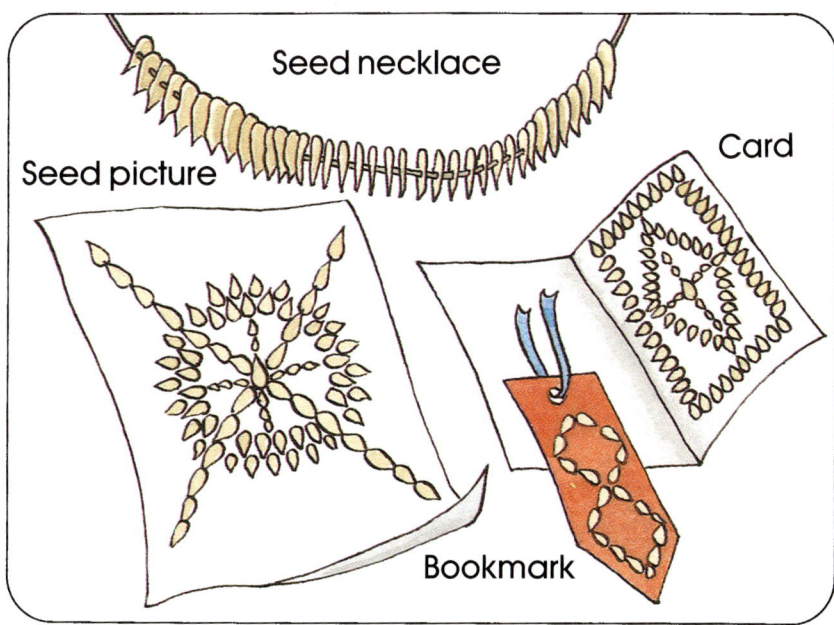

Seed necklace

Seed picture

Card

Bookmark

Glossary

Annual plants   Plants that grow, flower, release seeds and die in the course of a year.

Caribou   A North American animal closely related to the reindeer.

Chlorophyll   The substance which gives green plants their colour.

Citrus Fruits   Oranges, lemons, grapefruit and similar fruits.

Combine harvester   A machine for both cutting and threshing grain in one operation.

Cyclone   A violent storm moving with a circular motion.

Deciduous   A tree which sheds its leaves each year in autumn.

Dew   Tiny drops of water that cover the ground early in the morning after a cool night.

Equator   An imaginary line drawn around the centre of the earth halfway between the North and South Poles.

Equinox   A period, which occurs twice a year, when day and night are of equal length. One equinox marks the beginning of spring; the other equinox marks the beginning of autumn.

Hibernate   To spend the winter in a state similar to a deep sleep.

Hurricane   A storm with very violent winds, often moving with a circular motion.

Larvae   Insects which have hatched from eggs but which have not yet become pupae. Caterpillars are the larvae of butterflies.

Migrate   To move from one place to another, according to the season.

Northern hemisphere   The half of the world that lies north of the equator. It includes places such as Europe, Britain and North America.

Prune   To trim trees and bushes.

Pupae   Insects which are changing from larvae (such as caterpillars) to adults (such as butterflies). The insects do not move or feed during this stage and they are often wrapped in a cocoon.

Scythe   A long-handled, long-bladed implement for mowing cereals or grass.

Sickle   A short-handled hook with semi-circular blade for cutting or trimming vegetation.

Solstice   The periods when there is the greatest difference between the length of day and night. The summer solstice is the longest day of the year and the winter solstice is the shortest day of the year.

Southern hemisphere   The half of the world that lies south of the equator. It includes places such as Australia, New Zealand and southern Africa.

Synthetic   Manufactured; artificial.

Temperate zone   The part of the world having a mild climate, intermediate between a hot tropical climate and a cold polar climate.

Tundra   An immense grassy plain of cold regions, without trees and with a permanently frozen subsoil.

Typhoon   A violent storm, often circular in motion; the name is generally applied to storms over seas in eastern Asia.

Will-o'-the-wisp   A light like a pale flame seen in marshy areas. People used to think it was a lost spirit.

Further reading

Burton, Jane, **The Book of the Year** (Frederick Warne, 1983).

Doole, Louise Evans, **Herb Magic and Garden Craft** (Oak Tree Press, 1972).

Gerrard A. Peter, **Nature through the Seasons** (Midas Books, 1976).

Holden, Edith, **The Country Diary of an Edwardian Lady** (Webb & Bower, 1977).

Houghton, Graham, **Focus on Fruit** (Wayland, 1986).

Jenkings C. Alan, **A Countryman's Year** (Webb & Bower, 1980).

Kapoor Singh, Dr. Sukhbir, **Sikh Festivals** (Wayland, 1985).

Marsh, Janet, **Janet Marsh's Nature Diary** (Michael Joseph, 1979).

Mitter, Swasti, **Hindu Festivals** (Wayland, 1985).

Snelling, John, **Buddhist Festivals** (Wayland, 1985).

Vaughan-Thomas, Wynford, **The Countryside Companion** (Hutchison/Webb & Bower, 1979).

Whitlock, Ralph, **A Calendar of Country Customs** (Batsford, 1978).

Whitlock, Ralph **Harvest and Thanksgiving** (Wayland, 1984).

To study natural history, it is essential to have access to guidebooks which enable you to identify whatever you find. One of the most comprehensive series is Warne's series of Observer's books. These are small, practical books for identifying wild flowers, birds, butterflies, insects and life on the seashore.

Picture acknowledgements

The publishers would like to thank the following for allowing their photographs to be reproduced in this book: The Bridgeman Art Gallery 33; Cephas Picture Library 5, 21 (bottom); Bruce Coleman Limited 9 (bottom/John Shaw), 11 (top/Michael Freeman), 11 (bottom left/Gordon Langsbury), 13 (top/Jen and Des Bartlett), 13 (bottom/A.J. Deane), 15 (top/K. Wothe), 15 (bottom/Jeff Foott), 17 (Eric Crichton), 22 (Jonathan Wright), 23 (top/Eric Crichton), 26 (Frans Lanting), 27 (top/Frans Lanting), 29 (Jean-Jacques Joly), 37 (bottom/Keith Gunnar); Courtauld Institute Galleries, London (Courtauld Collection) 32 (bottom); E.T. Archive 32 (top); Geoscience Features Picture Library 14, 18, 27 (main picture), 28, 30; Jimmy Holmes, Himalayan Images 9 (top), 25 (bottom left); The Hutchison Library 4 (Constellaz), 10 (J.L. Peyromaure), 21 (top/Simon McBride), 23 (bottom/Bernard Gerard); 25 (bottom right); Tony Stone Worldwide *cover* (H. Richard Johnston); Wayland 7, 19, 36; ZEFA 11 (bottom right), 12, 25 (top), 37 (top). All the illustrations are by Ron Hayward Associates.

Index